Rules of Reason

Making and Evaluating Claims

Written By

BO BENNETT, PhD

http://www.rulesofreason.com

eBookIt.com
365 Boston Post Road, #311
Sudbury, MA 01776

First printing - May 2020

publishing@ebookit.com
http://www.ebookit.com

Copyright 2020, eBookIt.com
Ebook ISBN: 978-1-4566-3490-2
Print ISBN: 978-1-4566-3492-6
Published by eBookIt.com

Table of Contents

Preface

Back in 2012, after several years of being immersed in online debate for far more hours a day than I am proud to admit, I wrote the book, *Logically Fallacious*, which is like an encyclopedia of logical fallacies that identifies hundreds of common errors in reasoning. Since that time, I have been running the website of the same name where I help people from around the world parse arguments and identify if the arguments contain fallacies or not. What became clear is that identifying errors in reasoning will only get us so far to mastering reason. What is needed to get us all the way there are some rules to doing it right or *rules of reason*.

These rules of reason are unlike the immutable laws of logic. Laws reflect the way things are, whereas rules are more like guidelines that, when followed, consistently produce the most favorable outcome. Rules can be bent, and some even broken, especially in extenuating circumstances.

Think of these rules of reason like nutrition guidelines. Although nutrition guidelines are continually changing based on new information, the changes are relatively minor. It is highly unlikely that it will one day be discovered that we should be consuming twice as many calories or that fresh vegetables are bad for us, and we should be eating more Twinkies. We follow the general guidelines and make tweaks that work with our particular circumstances. Likewise, the rules of reason are the general guidelines to which tweaks can be made based on the particular circumstances.

This book contains the rules of reason for making and evaluating claims, which I believe to be an area where reason is most needed. Keep in mind that not all rules apply to all claims; some rules address certain kinds of claims, such as claims of causality and analogies. Properly and reasonably evaluating claims can have a dramatic impact on both your personal and professional life. Appealing to a higher cause, that cause being the stability of a democratic society, you can see it as your civic duty to do what you can to be an informed and responsible citizen. Knowing how to reason through claims should be knowledge taught in grade school.

Our goal in this book is to **evaluate the strength of claims, including the ones that we make.** We won't be going as far as to accept or reject claims, as that requires a deep understanding of evaluating evidence. But without a strong, clear, and well-presented claim, the evaluation of evidence can be a waste of time and even lead us to poor conclusions.

For evaluation purposes, we base the strength of a claim on how **clear** and **precise** it is, not how true it might be. The **strength of a claim** should not be confused with the **strength of an argument**, which includes one or more reasons for the claim. The claim "a living unicorn (i.e., the horse-like creature with a single horn from its head) is currently in my bedroom" is a strong claim despite the fact that it is almost certainly untrue.

In this book, we will be looking at eleven rules for making and evaluating claims, and going through many examples along the way. By the time you have finished this short book, no matter how good you were before at evaluating claims, I guarantee[1] that you will be even better at it.

---

[1] I don't mean a real guarantee like I will give you your money back or anything, just I am really confident about it and saying "guarantee" sounds really good.

Introduction

A *claim* is defined as a statement that something is the case, typically without being supported by evidence or proof. Unlike opinions, claims are independent of values and beliefs. The truth of the claim is unaffected by who makes the claim whether it be a staunch conservative or a life-long liberal. Consider this claim:

My husband is having sex with another woman.

If proof or convincing evidence was provided as part of the claim, the evaluation would be more of an exercise of validating the evidence, which is beyond the scope of this book. For the sake of comparison, however, let's look at this claim presented with evidence.

I caught my husband having sex with another woman. I recorded it and uploaded it on MyHusbandisaCheatingBastard.c om. I also uploaded a copy on MyHusbandsMistressisaTramp.co m. While I was at it, I added

Spanish subtitles and uploaded a copy to NoBuenoelEsposo.com.

When evidence is provided, reviewing the evidence is the "low-hanging fruit" of claim evaluation, meaning it is quite often the quickest and most accurate way to confirm that which was claimed to be the case is indeed the case. Too often, however, the wrong evidence is sought after based on a weak claim. Consider the following:

My husband is cheating on me with another woman. A woman at the nail salon mentioned that her husband's bowling buddy saw my husband talking closely for hours with a woman who wasn't me.

We can argue that this is not evidence for her husband cheating on her and the woman making the claim can argue that it is clear evidence, and we can both be right. The claim is weak because it is *ambiguous*; we don't know what "cheating" refers to in this case. The woman might be defining "cheating" as emotional intimacy with another person who is not family. We might define "cheating" as having sex with a person who is not your spouse. We should not focus on the evidence until we fully understand the claim.

Depending on the claim, good-quality evidence might not even be possible. If a claim is *falsifiable*, it means that evidence can exist that proves the claim to be false. For example,

> *"Anybody that wants a test can get a test. That's what the bottom line is."*

All it would take to falsify this claim is for someone, anyone, to want a test, attempt to get it, and fail.

Claims can also be *unfalsifiable*, which means no evidence can exist that would prove the claim to be false. Consider the following claim:

> *You can have anything you want as long as you want it badly enough!*

Through probability alone, some people will get what they want, and some people won't. Those who get what they want lend support to this claim and those who don't either just didn't get it yet since no timeframe was specified or it can be claimed that they simply didn't want it badly enough, in either case, not taking away from the credibility of the claim. This is what gives staying power to such claims and make unfalsifiable claims prime drivers of pseudoscience, marketing scams, and religions.

Sometimes, the probability of claims being true is not mathematically calculable; that is, their probabilities are unknowable. Recall that our goal in this book is only to evaluate the strength of the claim and not how likely the claim is to be true. But we do need to briefly look at how an unknown probability affects the veracity of the claim. Consider the following claim:

Jesus was raised from the dead.

The fact is, we have zero proven or demonstrated cases of anyone ever being raised from the dead, but many claimed cases. Given this, we can't calculate the percent chance that Jesus was raised from the dead. We can use what is called *Bayesian statistics* to estimate a probability, but this requires initial assumptions that make the estimated percent highly susceptible to bias. When we can't calculate a probability, we can still compare claims to competing claims and make use of the *principle of parsimony* to choose the more reasonable claim.

Consider the following claims:

1. The God of the Bible created the universe.

2. There was some god who created the universe.

3. Something caused the universe to come into existence.

Note that there is no reason all three claims can't be true. Just because they are *competing* doesn't mean they are *contradicting*. Although we cannot calculate the probabilities of any of these claims, we know that statistically, claim #3 contains the fewest assumptions and is, therefore, most likely to be true. Claim #2 contains claim #3, plus it adds all of the properties of what a "god" is. Claim #1 contains claims #2 and #3, plus all of the properties as written in the Bible. Even though it is more likely that "something" caused the universe to come into existence than "the God of the Bible" created the universe, the claim that "something" caused the universe to come into existence is not very helpful and somewhat pointless, which is why we often sacrifice probability for a more specific claim.

Now that you have a decent primer on the issues with claims let's get into the eleven rules of reason for making and evaluating claims.

Know Thyself

Reasoning is a process that is strongly influenced by many factors that are not easily apparent to us. Both biology and environment shape who we are and how we think. While we are not in complete control of our intellect and reasoning, we do have some control, and we can get even more control by knowing our cognitive limitations and keeping those limitations in mind when making and evaluating claims.

Rule #1: Acknowledge the Limits of Your Knowledge Regarding the Claim

It has been said that a little knowledge is a dangerous thing, and the advent of the Internet has certainly provided us with many examples where this is true. Keyboard warriors who spend a few hours on Google and YouTube convince themselves that they know more than doctors, researchers, scientists, and academics who spend their lives studying a narrow field where they have attained mastery. Even the doctors, researchers, scientists, and academics can convince themselves that they know far more than they do. We all need to acknowledge the limits of our knowledge.

We don't know what we don't know, or to put another way, without knowing how much there is to know about a particular topic, we have no way to know how much about that topic we do know. Unfortunately for us, we grossly overestimate our knowledge and competence. This is a well-known effect in psychology, known as the *Dunning-Kruger effect*. The good news is, if we realize that we are likely to be victims of this effect, we can take this into consideration and lower our estimate of how much we actually know. Once we have an accurate assessment of our knowledge on the topic, we can identify and defer to people who know more than we do on the topic. When we realize that there is still more we can learn on the topic; we will be less resistant to related information that could increase our understanding of the topic.

Even if you are confident in your level of knowledge on the topic, realize that factual information or good advice can come from those people and sources less knowledgeable than you on the topic. Dismissing information solely on the source, although reasonable at times depending on the source and situation, is a fallacy known as the *genetic fallacy*. To illustrate this point, just think about a time when someone tried to "educate" you on a topic about which you actually knew far more they did. You probably felt that they were patronizing or that they were ignorant, and as a result, resisted the information they shared. What you might not have realized at the time is that even if the information they presented was factually correct or a good suggestion, your convictions of you being right led you to dismiss the factually correct information over the preservation of your believed "rightness." The result... you missed an opportunity to become even more knowledgeable on the topic, not to mention, you almost certainly appeared ignorant to the other person.

Rule Summary: Understand that there is likely much you don't know on the topic and realize that even sources that are frequently wrong are sometimes right.

Rule #2: Explore Your Biases Related to the Claim

Raised as a Catholic, I attended religious school from the third grade until the eighth-grade and remained a believer well into my thirties. In high school, I had a friend who was an atheist. He would often present arguments as to why the God I believed in almost certainly didn't exist. I remember, at the time, being terrified because his arguments made sense. I also remember believing that if I didn't believe in God, I would spend eternity being tortured in Hell, not to mention upset the God that was responsible for all the good things in my life. I defended my belief in God just as passionately as I would defend my own life —because, in a way, I was.

Cognitive psychologists refer to what I experienced as *motivated reasoning*, an extremely powerful phenomenon where our reasoning process is hijacked by our desires. I wasn't pretending; I wasn't lying; I was authentically arguing what I believed because what I believed was strongly influenced by my emotions, not reason.

When we have a vested interest in the outcome, many cognitive biases kick in and distort our reasoning. This creates a dilemma. On the one hand, passion could be a wonderful force that energizes us to cause change for good. On the other hand, passion can blind us to facts and reality when facts and reality contradict our ideological positions. There is a solution. The solution is to be passionate about discovering truth. Be passionate about learning, logic, and reason, no matter where it leads.

In a generic sense and in the context of reasoning, a *bias* is a tendency to favor select information in an unreasonable manner, usually due to emotion interfering with reason. The reason why you personally may have these powerful emotional biases are best left for a therapist; you just need to be able to notice them, which is generally not difficult because they accompany strong emotion rather than indifference. For example, if you ever felt an immediate sense of frustration when calling technical support and being connected to a woman, this is a bias. This isn't about sexism; it is about having a preconceived notion that men are better at technical issues than women. Okay, maybe it is about sexism.

A *cognitive bias* is a systematic error in thinking that affects the decisions and judgments that people make. These are much more difficult to detect than our standard biases for several reasons. First, most of these errors are not the result of strong emotion, so there is no visceral indicator of the bias. Second, there are literally hundreds of known biases, which makes memorizing them challenging, to say the least. And third, there is actually a cognitive bias that prevents us from readily admitting our cognitive biases know as the *bias blind spot*. Despite these challenges, we can recognize our own biases with a cursory knowledge of the biases and some practice. Did I mention that I have an online course on cognitive biases at w w w . v i r v e r s i t y . c o m / c o u r s e / cognitivebiases?

Here are just a handful of what I have found to be the most common cognitive biases people experience related to evaluating claims along with suggestions on how you can overcome these biases.

- **Confirmation Bias.** People choose news sources that are most likely to report information that is consistent with what they already believe. Likewise, they dismiss or even subconsciously forget information that contradicts their beliefs. A near-perfect example of this is how President Trump refers to news that is hostile to him as "Fake News." This label of "fake" is independent of the truth value of the claims made by the source, but rather a result of agreeing with President Trump. To combat the confirmation bias, focus on facts and reality, not on being right. Embrace being wrong; don't deny it.

- **Courtesy Bias.** This is the tendency to agree with a claim because it is the polite thing to do, not because you actually agree with the claim. This is a problem because it gives the appearance that the claim is supported by far more people than it actually is (not that the number of people who support the claim makes it any more true). If the goal is to accurately assess the probability of a claim, agreeing with the claim just to be "nice" is antithetical to the goal. I can't tell you how many times I read my Facebook friend's posts and cringe. In most cases, I make the conscious decision not to engage, which is fine. This is displaying judgment and diplomacy. This is a problem when similar claims are made in friendly discussion or debate, and we don't cringe; rather, we find ourselves nodding in acceptance or even just accepting the claim in an unconscious attempt to avoid conflict. To combat the courtesy bias, remind yourself frequently that good people can and do say stupid things.

- **Groupthink.** This is a psychological phenomenon that occurs within a group of people in which the desire for harmony or conformity in the group results in an irrational or dysfunctional decision-making outcome. The ideal example exists in virtually all Facebook groups, especially ones conducive to strong ideological positions. Imagine you are in a group for liberal politics. A member posts an anti-conservative meme that is instantly liked and supported by the community. As comments start to roll in, they become more extreme to the point of dysfunctional reasoning. The power of the group norm nudges the average group member in the direction of unreason. This is where the term "ideological bubble" comes from and why networks like MSNBC and FOX News tend to get more polarized. To combat groupthink, you need to think of yourself as an individual and an arbiter of reason when in group environments.

- **Overconfidence Effect**. This is perhaps the most devastating bias when it comes to accepting facts and reason. It is the idea that you are far more confident in the accuracy of your claims then you should be, based on the measured accuracy of those claims. Researchers did many experiments where they would ask people about a belief they held that could be demonstrably verified, and asked them how confident they were that the claim was true. The researchers found that, on average, when people were 100% confident they were wrong 20% of the time. If we think we are "certain" about anything, then why bother considering that we might be wrong? We don't. And that's a problem. Maintain a healthy level of skepticism about your own level of confidence.

- **Halo / Pitchfork Effects**. This is the tendency for an impression created in one area to influence opinion in another area. The *Halo effect* is a positive impression, and the *Pitchfork effect* is a negative impression. Once again, we can turn to President Trump, arguably the most polarizing political figure in history, for an example of this cognitive bias in action. However, this time, we can look at those who despise Trump. If President Trump makes what would typically be seen as a non-partisan decision, say increasing subsidies on school lunches, we see that a disturbing number of Trump haters will find some reason to be outraged, not because of the decision, but because it was Trump who made the decision. Substitute Obama with Trump and Obama haters with Trump haters, and we see the same phenomenon. Clearly, this is an abandonment of reason and another example of passion (negative or positive) interfering with the reasoning process. Do your best to separate the claim from the source making the claim.

- **Stereotyping**. When we hold an over-generalized belief about a particular group or class of people, we are *stereotyping*. Stereotyping is similar to the generic use of "bias" we discussed earlier in that we are biased against a group to which the person making the claim belongs. For example, if we hold the stereotype that Irishmen are less intelligent than other groups, and an Irishman is making a claim, we are likely to irrationally devalue the legitimacy of the claim even if it is independent of the person making the claim. To combat stereotyping in the context of evaluating claims, remember to separate the claim from the source.

The idea that we should consider the source when evaluating a claim is a controversial one. On the one hand, a claim would ideally be evaluated on its own merit. Reliable sources are wrong at times, and unreliable sources are right at times. Considering the credibility of the source can significantly sway the outcome of our evaluation, especially if our biases go unchecked. On the other hand, considering the source can serve as a useful and accurate heuristic, in that by taking this mental shortcut we can probabilistically be right more times than we are wrong. If a quick evaluation is called for, evaluating the source may be the best course of action, but if we have the time and are looking to do a thorough evaluation of the claim, we need to ignore the source, at least initially. Factoring the historical reliability of the source in the overall evaluation can help if the probability of the claim is otherwise unknowable.

Rule Summary: Explore your biases and realize when they might be affecting your judgment.

Disambiguate

Once we have our biases under control, we can look at the claim in detail and parse all relevant terms in an attempt to remove as much ambiguity as possible through a general process called *disambiguation*. With the next several rules, we will cover specific forms of disambiguation, starting with isolating the actual claim being made.

Rule #3: Isolate the Actual Claim

If there were a way to calculate the number of hours people waste online arguing over a claim that was never made, we would find that the number is... big. The *strawman*, or a logical fallacy where one presents a version of an argument not made but one that is easier to refute, is one of the more common fallacies. We want to avoid this fallacy and fully understand the true meaning of the claim, which often involves asking for clarification.

In the age of Googling, it seems like people are more hesitant to make explicit, unambiguous claims. So it is our job to *isolate* the claim or parse what is often a rant, meme, or some other combination of words and answer the question, "what exactly is the claim here?" This is surprisingly challenging because we often make subconscious assumptions to fill in the blanks. The result is that we think we are clear what the claim is, but we are really not. If we are lucky, we can ask for clarification and get it. But sometimes, we need to do our best with what we have.

We can categorize claims in two broad categories: *explicit* and *implicit* claims. An explicit claim is a direct claim or declaration. Some examples:

The sun is about 93,000,000 miles from the earth.

The earth is flat.

People who think the earth is flat are idiots.

Implicit claims are claims that are not directly stated but implied. Some examples:

We don't want no Muslim as our president! (double negative intended to communicate ignorance)

Back in the 1950s, kids knew the value of hard work.

Are you really going to wear that?

Notice these statements don't make any direct claims, but most people can "read between the lines" to figure out what is being suggested. The statement "We don't want no Muslim as our president," assuming said during the Obama administration, appears to be suggesting that Obama is a Muslim. The statement "Back in the 1950s, kids knew the value of hard work," appears to be suggesting that kids today do not know the value of hard work. The question "Are you really going to wear that?" appears to be suggesting that they shouldn't wear what they are wearing. Notice the phrase "appears to be suggesting." With implicit claims, there is a greater margin of error involved in parsing the claim, which is why we are careful to convey that uncertainty in our language. Avoid telling people what they mean; let **them tell you** what they mean by asking them what they are suggesting. If we have access to the person making the claim, we should do what we can to make the implicit, explicit, which will eliminate that margin of error.

Rule Summary: Isolate the claim by finding out exactly what is meant by the claim. This will often uncover an implicit claim.

Rule #4: Clearly and Precisely Define Each Relevant Term

Now that we have isolated the actual claim and made the implicit, explicit, we can clearly and precisely define each relevant term to help us gain an accurate understanding of the claim being made.

Climate change is a hoax!

The relevant terms here are "climate change" and "hoax." Climate change is a very broad topic that contains one or more of the following claims:

1. The earth's temperature is rising (uncontroversial)

2. Human activities are the primary reason for the rise in temperature (more controversial)

3. We need to take extreme measures now to fight climate change (most controversial)

"Hoax" can mean anything from "not a real thing" to malicious deception carefully organized and executed by some group or cabal. Again, asking for clarification is how we make the claim as precise as possible. On the two extremes, we can either have:

The earth's temperature is not rising, and all data showing otherwise is the result of malicious deception carefully organized and executed by some group or cabal.

or

The media exaggerates the likely consequences of not taking the extreme measures suggested regarding climate change.

As you can see, these two claims are quite different even though the initial, more generic claim is the same for both. Removing as much ambiguity as possible goes a long way in effective communication.

Rule Summary: Words have multiple meanings, and people use them differently. Don't guess the meaning if you have the opportunity to get clarification. Clearly and precisely define each relevant term in the claim.

Rule #5: Use Terms That Reflect the Scope and Degree of the Claim Accurately

As suggested previously, it seems to be a common practice of deception to make a claim without actually making a claim, therefore, not having to defend the claim. We have seen this so far with implicit claims, ambiguous claims, and will see it with claims that express possibility (incorrectly). Deception (deliberate or not) can result from omitting from the claim the *scope,* or the extent to which the claim applies. Deception, usually more deliberate, comes from misrepresenting the degree of the claim, typically indicated by an inaccurate scope or the misuse of superlatives.

Let's first look at an example of omitting the scope.

All men are bastards.

Some men are bastards.

Men are bastards.

Assuming we clearly define "bastards" and disambiguate "man" (including specify if we are referring to to those currently alive or all that ever lived or will live), the first claim would be the easiest to falsify. The scope covers all members of the group "men." All it would take is to present one man who doesn't meet the established measured criteria of "bastard" to falsify the claim. The second claim is functionally impossible to falsify because one would have to evaluate the "bastard-ness" of every man, but thanks to the *burden of proof*, the one making the claim has the responsibility to demonstrate the claim to be true rather than us having to demonstrate the claim false. Regardless, and I think many women would agree, demonstrating that "some men are bastards" is not difficult. The problem arises when we fail to specify a scope, as in the last claim, "men are bastards." Are we talking all men? Some? Most? Many? Even those words are wishy-washy (technical term), and if possible, we want to state claims and understand claims in terms of probability:

In my estimation, based on personal experience and extrapolating to the population, about 30% of men are bastards.

Of course, this isn't without its problems, but it's a significant improvement from the "men are bastards" claim.

Consider the following claim made by President Trump about the COVID-19 pandemic in March of 2020:

*This is a very contagious -- this is a very contagious virus. It's incredible. But it's something that we have **tremendous control** of.*[2]

Although Trump's use of "very contagious" is an appropriate representation of the relative degree of contagiousness, his use of "tremendous control of" was clearly an inaccurate representation of the relative degree over which we had control of the virus at the time. Inaccurate representations of the relative degree of control we had over the virus was found on the other side as well, just at the other extreme. USA Today wrote the following regarding President Trump:

*He has **no control** over the virus as it threatens the USA, supporters noted, and must exude*

---

[2] https://www.whitehouse.gov/briefings-statements/remarks-president-trump-vice-president-pence-members-coronavirus-task-force-press-briefing-2/

*confidence that the nation will get
through it.*[3]

How much control do we have over the
virus? There is an overwhelming consensus
within the medical community that we do
have some level of control over COVID-19,
thus the social distancing guidelines,
lockdowns, hand-washing, and other
recommended behaviors. Many models
predicted that without taking these
measures, many more people were likely to
die due to exceeding peak healthcare
demand. Still, the extreme of "tremendous
control of" is inaccurate. We have
"tremendous control of" polio—at least
within the United States.

Dr. Fauci was the voice of reason when,
in an April 5th press conference, he was
asked if this virus is under control:

*I will not say we have it under
control, Margaret. That would be
a false statement. We are
struggling to get it under control,*

[3] https://www.usatoday.com/story/news/politics/
2020/03/10/coronavirus-trump-shifts-message-crisis-
grows-stocks-plummet/4966450002/

and that's the issue that's at hand right now.[4]

We don't have to choose between "tremendous control" and "no control." As it is overwhelmingly the case, the truth lies between the extremes.

Rule Summary: To avoid ambiguity, specify the scope of the claim. Use words like "all," "none," "a few," "some," and "many." When possible, be even more specific by providing numbers or percentages.

---

[4] https://thehill.com/homenews/sunday-talk-shows/
491228-fauci-says-it-would-be-false-statement-to-say-we-
have-coronavirus

Rule #6: Operationalize Terms When Possible

In science, the term *operationalize* refers to defining a term in such a way to make it measurable. For example, if we want to know if being isolated contributes to depression, we need to operationalize both "isolation" as well as "depression." What counts as isolation? Being alone? Just being with family? For how long? With Internet access? How do we measure depression? When it comes to mental illness, there are many *assessment instruments* that are used to accurately measure such psychological states. For example, the *Beck Depression Inventory (BDI)*, a common way to measure depression, contains 21 self-report items that individuals complete using multiple-choice response formats. But for everyday claims, we don't need to be so technical; **we just need to establish some benchmark by which we can tell how true the claim is.**

Consider the following claim:

100,000 Americans will die due to COVID-19.

This claim has already been isolated, and as far as ambiguity goes, it is clear what is being claimed. However, we do need to operationalize deaths due to COVID-19. At the time of this writing, measuring deaths due to COVID-19 has been both inconsistent and inaccurate. There are claims that many people have died in their homes of COVID-19 and were not counted. There are also claims that a "COVID-19-related death" is recorded if the person was tested positive for COVID-19 at the time of death, regardless if the virus caused the death or not. The key aspect of operationalization is not choosing a way to measure with which everyone agrees but just choosing a way to measure. Unlike disambiguation, the criteria by which we measure are not easily inserted into the claim itself. Rather, we need to expand upon the claim.

100,000 Americans will die due to COVID-19. Death is measured by the official numbers reported by the CDC.

The reason we don't need full agreement on the measurement, is that we can evaluate claims using multiple measurements and if/then statements:

If death is measured by the official numbers reported by the

CDC, then 100,000 Americans will die due to COVID-19. However, if we account for all those who have died of other causes who also happened to test positive for COVID-19, then the number of Americans who actually died from the disease will be closer to 70,000.[5]

Operationalization is very useful with *loaded language* or rhetoric used to influence an audience by using words and phrases with strong connotations associated with them in order to invoke an emotional response and/or exploit stereotypes.[6] Consider a situation where a man put his hand on a woman's lower back when the woman was in pain and asked her if she was okay. If the woman claimed:

I was sexually assaulted. He was caressing my lower back without my consent.

We need to operationalize "sexual assault" and disambiguate "caress." Here is where a

---

[5] This example is for illustration purposes only and does not represent an accurate claim of COVID-19 deaths.

[6] Weston, Anthony (2000). A Rulebook for Arguments. Hackett Publishing. p. 6. ISBN 978-0-87220-552-9.

technique I call the *Reductio Ad Consequentia*[7] can play a valuable role in claim evaluation. When we operationalize "sexual assault," if we make the criteria for "sexual assault" too strict, then the consequences would be that other actions that most would agree constitute sexual assault would no longer fit under "sexual assault." If we make the criteria too loose, then the consequences would be that other actions most would not see as sexual assault, would constitute "sexual assault." This exercise can help the parties involved agree on the criteria or it may result in the claim being modified (e.g., "He made me feel uncomfortable by touching my lower back.") If it has not been clear by now how important evaluating claims are, this example should make it clear. The modified claim would justify a sincere apology where the original claim would justify a prison sentence.

The word "caress" is one that can imply intention. It is defined as "touch or stroke gently or lovingly." We would want to resolve the ambiguity because a "gentle touch" is quite different from a "loving stroke." We must be cautious of claims that infer intention of a third party since the one

---

[7] https://www.hostingauthors.com/posts/bobennett/
reductio_ad_consequentia___reducing_the_argument_to_
the_consequences.html

making the claim doesn't have access to that person's thoughts and when the intentions were not clearly communicated. We might find that the claim would be more accurate and precise if we replaced "caress" with "moved his hand in a circular motion."

It is quite easy to alter the intended meaning of ambiguous claims with a little wordsmithing fueled by ideological bias. There is a reason that there are thousands of Christian denominations all based on the same book. The Bible is the Holy Grail of ambiguous claims and a good example of how easy it is to change the meaning of a claim. Networks with known biases such as MSNBC and Fox News can take the same quote from Donald Trump and come to wildly different interpretations. In cases where the claims were written thousands of years ago, or claims are made by people who are not readily accessible for providing clarifications, the best we can do is evaluate the claim in the context they were made, taking into account the source of the claim and all available background information.

Rule Summary: For terms that can be measured, ask how they can be measured so the claim can be investigated using one ore more reasonable standards.

Rule #7: Make the Claim Falsifiable When Possible

Ideally, a claim can be falsified or able to be demonstrated to be wrong. A falsifiable claim does not guarantee a strong claim, but an unfalsifiable claim does limit the strength of the claim. Consider the following claims:

The world will end on December 21, 2012.

The world will end after 1000 years of peace.

The world will end when God wants it to end, and only he knows when that will be.

The first claim is falsifiable, assuming December 21, 2012, has passed or is within a reasonable amount of time from when the claim is being evaluated. If December 21, 2012, has passed and we're still here (we are), then the claim was demonstrated to be false. We would have successfully evaluated a claim with 100% probability, and we are all the wiser. The second claim, however, is what we might call *functionally* unfalsifiable in that we cannot falsify the claim in our lifetimes, but perhaps the human race will be around long enough to falsify it (after operationalizing "peace"). The third claim is just plain unfalsifiable since, assuming there is a God, there is no way to know when God would want the world to end as made clear in the claim. Unfalsifiable claims are often dead-ends in the claim evaluation process because we simply cannot determine how probable the claim is. What we can do is attempt to make the claim falsifiable.

Making an unfalsifiable claim, falsifiable, requires the person who made the claim to revise the claim in such a way that it is falsifiable. Consider the second claim that the world will end after 1000 years of peace. We might ask the person making the claim how they know this. They might reference the book of Revelation and how it comes from an "infallible" book (the Bible). Now we have a falsifiable claim to work with. If we can show that the Bible does contain claims that are false or even claims that aren't meant to be taken literally, we may get the person to revise or even retract their initial claim.

A note of caution. Don't overestimate the ease of convincing others that you have falsified their claim. Remember the concept of motivated reasoning—if someone desperately wants to believe a claim is true, there are many ways they can rationalize the claim as still being true. Making a strong argument against a claim and convincing a neutral audience is one thing, convincing a highly-motivated person who made the claim is something else.

Rule Summary: Do your best to modify the claim so that it is possible to be demonstrated to be false. Otherwise, it will likely be a weak claim.

Rule #8: Express an Accurate and Meaningful Level of Confidence

One of the admirable traits of a good leader is said to be their confidence. Confidence and certainty are generally seen as positive qualities, while doubt and uncertainty are generally seen as negative qualities—in leaders. When it comes to critical thinking and reason, the reverse is true. Doubt, skepticism, and uncertainty are the hallmark of critical thought where confidence and certainty are often associated with cognitive biases that thwart the reasoning process. When claims are made, they are often made with either an inflated level of confidence as expressed in the way the claim is stated or an unhelpful and virtually meaningless air of possibility. Consider the following claim made in the summer of 2016, several months prior to the U.S. presidential election:

Hillary Clinton will win the 2016 presidential election.

This claim can either be interpreted as unclear or unreasonable. If the person who made the claim really believed that there was a 95% chance Clinton would win, they are just being unclear when making the claim, and making an inaccurate claim—one that neither represents reality nor their belief. If they actually were 100% confident that Clinton would win, they were unreasonable holding that level of confidence for what was clearly a less probable outcome.

Now consider this claim:

It is possible that 2 million Americans will die from COVID-19.

The phrase "it is possible that" makes the claim virtually meaningless. Before we get into why exactly, a philosophical diversion is needed. Rather than saying, "anything is possible," we should say, "we don't know if something is possible or impossible until we demonstrate its possibility or impossibility. Until such time, we say that the possibility is unknown." This is more important when you are the one making the claim, but it is also helpful to point out to others who claim possibility or impossibility when that hasn't been demonstrated. For example, the fine-tuning argument for God's existence argues that the variables that make the conditions for life possible are so precise that if any were off by a fraction of what they are, life wouldn't exist. Ignoring all other problems with this argument, the fact is that we don't know that it is possible that the variables could have been anything other than what they are—we can't simply assert that they could have been different. That would need to be demonstrated. This doesn't mean it is impossible for the variables to have been different; it simply means that the possibility is unknown.

I mentioned that the phrase "it is possible that" makes the claim virtually meaningless. We can add to that list words and phrases such as "can," "may," "might," "could," "there's a chance," "it's not impossible," and others that express the same idea. These statements have some meaning when the possibility has been established and demonstrated. For example:

After years of testing, we found that it is possible to cause impotence by placing photos of grandma on the nightstand.

The phrase establishing possibility here is used differently than how it was used in the COVID-19 example. In the COVID-19 example, it was used as a possible future, something we cannot possibly know. In the impotence example, the possibility has been demonstrated.

The other point that makes these kinds of possibility claims virtually meaningless and not completely meaningless is that they are often used as a tool for persuasion as well as manipulation. People who say "You know, climate change could be a hoax," aren't saying that for no reason; they are saying that to instill doubt, communicating that they are not confident that climate change is a real problem, or perhaps they're just watching too much Fox News. The point is, we need to get to the actual claim being made.

A Note on Plausibility

Plausibility differs from probability in that plausibility is about one's level of belief or what seems reasonable to the person expressing the plausibility, whereas probability is a mathematical concept that is not based on the whims of one's beliefs, but rather based on objective data. Consider the claim:

It's plausible that ghosts exist.

What this means is that the person making the claim thinks ghosts existing is a reasonable conclusion. This isn't a claim about the probability or the likelihood of ghosts existing, although the person making this claim might not know the difference. When making claims, think about the differences between possibility, probability, and plausibility and use the correct term. When evaluating claims, verify, if possible, if the person making the claim is using the right term.

Rule Summary: Make sure claims reflect an accurate, clear, and meaningful level of confidence.

Embrace the Continuum

It goes by many names: *black and white thinking, all or nothing mindset, dichotomous thinking, polarized thinking, binary thinking,* and *splitting.* All these terms represent the tendency to think in extremes. We all dip our toes into this way of thinking from time to time, but for some, this habit of thinking can lead to poor life outcomes and is associated with several kinds of mental illness including depression, PTSD, and Borderline Personality Disorder (BPD).[8] What this means is that this tendency to think in extremes could be just lazy thinking for some people and a deeply ingrained habit for others. And of course, there are many who fall between these extremes. In the context of reason, I prefer the term "binary thinking," which is considered a cognitive distortion because it distorts our complex and nuanced reality into a simplistic one of right or wrong and good or bad. How do you feel about conservatives? How do you feel about liberals? How do you feel about

---

[8] https://www.betterhelp.com/advice/personality-disorders/how-black-and-white-thinking-affects-you/

Christians? How do you feel about atheists? Reflect on those questions for a moment. If you find yourself feeling strong emotions about an entire group, the chances are that you are engaged in binary thinking. If this is the case, refer to rule #2.

Rule #9: Convert Causes to Contributing Factors When Appropriate

Having a decent understanding of causality can go a long way towards better reasoning. Binary thinking is frequently reflected in claims of causality. Consider the following claims:

The reason the economy suffers is because of lazy citizens who prefer handouts to working.

The reason there is so much violent crime is that humans are violent by nature.

Bill's car was stolen because he parked in a sketchy neighborhood.

Trump is to blame for the high number of COVID-19 fatalities in the U.S.

The key to success is persistence!

What all of these claims have in common is a simplistic "reason" given for what is, in reality, a complex series of cause and effect comprising many contributing factors. More reasonable ways to make the above claims would go as follows:

> ***One of the reasons*** *the economy suffers is because* ***some citizens*** *who are lazy prefer handouts to working.*

> *Humanity's violent nature is a* ***clear contributor*** *to the level of violent crime we see in the world today.*

> ***One of the reasons*** *Bill's car was stolen was because he parked it in a sketchy neighborhood.*

> *Trump's inaction and casual attitude, especially at the start of the pandemic,* ***undoubtedly contributed*** *to the high number of COVID-19 fatalities in the U.S.*

> *Persistence is consistently identified as* ***one of the leading contributors*** *of success by successful individuals.*

Evaluating and making scientific claims, especially ones that establish or suggest causation, require a higher standard of evidence and precision not met by the revised examples just given. However, for making and evaluating casual claims, remembering to think in terms of contributing factors rather than the binary idea of "a cause" can go a long way towards being more reasonable.

Rule Summary: Causality is a complex area that is virtually always better expressed in terms of causal factors than "the cause," "the reason," "the key," or other terms that indicate a binary distinction.

Rule #10: Make Strong Analogies and Call Out Weak Ones

The analogy is one of the most useful tools in argumentation, as well as one of the most helpful aids in effective reasoning. It allows us to compare something with which we are familiar to something with which we are unfamiliar, then use the similarities to check for consistency in our reasoning. But thanks to our stubbornness, our refusal to be wrong, and our allegiance to ideology over reason, we flippantly dismiss analogies that don't support our position by labeling them "weak analogies" or "false equivalence," robbing ourselves of the opportunity to grow intellectually.

There is no "rule" stating that things cannot be compared—for any reason. During the COVID-19 pandemic, it was common to hear people parrot the politically-correct mantra that we cannot compare COVID-19 to the flu, then continue by comparing the two saying something such as "COVID-19 is far more deadly." When people say "you can't compare..." what they often mean is "after comparing, I find stark differences." No analogy is off-limits, not even comparing someone to Hitler. Comparing is not the same as equating.

Here are some key points to consider when making or evaluating analogies.

1) All analogies are different in some way from that to which it is being compared. If they weren't, it wouldn't be an analogy. However, a strong analogy might say how two similar things are equivalent in some specific way. Here is where committing the *false equivalence* fallacy becomes a possibility. This is an argument or claim in which two completely opposing arguments appear to be logically equivalent when, in fact they are not. The confusion is often due to one shared characteristic between two or more items of comparison in the argument that is way off in the order of magnitude, oversimplified, or just that important additional factors have been ignored. The false equivalence fallacy requires a claim of equivalence, usually identified by the phrases "no different than," "same as," or similar language establishing "sameness." Consider the following example,

President Petutti ordered a military strike that killed many civilians. He is no different than any other mass murderer, and he belongs in prison!

While it is the case that both President Petutti and mass murderers share the characteristic "ultimately responsible for the deaths of many civilians," the (implied) claim is that they share the same legal culpability, which is not the case.

2) Analogies that are ambiguous are not good analogies. Very often, one will make an analogy and not be clear as to why what is being compared is similar. If I said apples are like oranges, and just left it there, confusion would ensue. In some ways, apples are like oranges, and in some ways, they are not. By simply adding why they are alike, we can solve this ambiguity problem. "Apples are like oranges in that they are both fruits." One can be deliberately ambiguous to avoid having to justify their analogy and just make a statement that has a powerful emotional impact. For example,

A vote for Trump is like a vote to end democracy as we know it!

Okay, but **why** is a vote for Trump like a vote to end democracy? By not providing a reason for how the two are similar, we leave it up to the imaginations of the audience. This is wholly unhelpful because pro-Trump folks would simply disagree. This is like just stating a conclusion without providing any premises. If your goal is to get support from those who already agree with you, fine, but if your goal is to convince people who don't agree with you, you must remove the ambiguity and connect the dots for the audience by telling them how the two are alike. You might list the ways in which Trump has interfered with democracy, then compare how this is a significant change from how democracy has changed under other presidents. If you fail to make your case, you may be called out on a *weak analogy*.

3) Analogies that are weak are not good analogies and considered fallacious. When an analogy is used to prove or disprove an argument, but the analogy is too dissimilar to be effective, that is, it is unlike the argument more than it is like the argument, then we call this a weak analogy (or weak analogy fallacy). Ambiguous analogies are often weak because the entirety of two things is being compared rather than a specific characteristic shared by the two things. The vote-for-Trump analogy could be reasonably argued to fall somewhere on the weak to strong continuum. If you want to virtually ensure you are making a strong analogy (and not a fallaciously weak one), be specific and clear in your analogy by answering how or in what way the two things being compared are similar. For example,

If we should implement stop and frisk because it "saves lives," then by the same reasoning, we should ban cars because that would undoubtedly save lives.

Here we are comparing implementing two policies: stop and frisk and banning cars. We are saying they are similar in that they both save lives. It is in that regard, and only in that regard that the comparison is being made. Clearly, there is a sense of irony in this argument. The person is not seriously suggesting that we should ban cars, but the implication is that just "saving lives" is not a sufficient reason to implement a policy. This is effectively an *argumentum ad absurdum* (i.e., suggesting that implementing a policy just because it "saves lives" leads to absurd conclusions when we apply this to other possible policies).

Analogies and Claims

Most analogies are claims. If the analogy is specific in how the two things are similar, and it is true that they are both similar in that regard, you should accept the analogy with its limitation (i.e., the claim is that the two things are analogous in regards to the specific shared feature only). If the analogy fails to be specific and fails to clearly state or even clearly imply how the two things being compared are similar, and there are more differences between the two than similarities (or the similarities differ significantly in degree), then you reject the analogy as a weak analogy. For example, "Believing in God is like believing in Santa Claus," can generally be regarded as a weak analogy. One can make a list of hundreds of properties of God and Santa, and the differences (in number and degree) would clearly exceed the similarities. In order to strengthen such an analogy, we might say something such as "God is like Santa Claus in that both God and Santa are represented as old white guys with long grey hair and beards who are said to see you when you're sleeping, know when your awake, and know when you've been bad or good."

Accepting and rejecting analogies is a binary distinction, just like the ones I warned against. So what gives? Here is where the concept of a *threshold* comes in. If you think about it, it makes no sense that a twenty-one-year-old is allowed to drink alcohol, but someone who is twenty and 364 days old could get arrested for it. Twenty-one is the threshold for the legal drinking age that was determined. It's not arbitrary nor random; it is based on many factors and decades of data. Likewise, decisions often have to be made based on claims, decisions that necessitate a binary choice of action vs. no action. We avoid the problem of binary thinking by accepting or rejecting analogies with the level of confidence justified by the quality of the analogy. For example, if someone makes an analogy that just passes our threshold of being fallacious and therefore rejecting, we wouldn't tell them that their analogy was "horrible," and spend hours arguing against it.

You should treat every analogy presented to you as a learning experience. Ask how what is being compared are similar, as well as how they are different. In the ways they are the same, are they the same but in significantly different ways (e.g., President Petutti may be responsible for the deaths of many innocent civilians just like a psychotic mass murderer, but the reasons behind the deaths are significantly different enough to make the claim of equivalence fallacious). Is the claim of similarity specified, or is it left ambiguous (therefore, generic)? Does the analogy work as a legitimate reductio ad absurdum that points out a flaw in your reasoning?

Analogies are extremely useful tools that every critical thinker should have at their disposal. They can be quite persuasive, but they can also be quite deceptive. Use them, don't abuse them, and learn to spot when others are abusing them by considering analogies carefully before dismissing them as fallacious or simply accepting them because they are ideologically pleasing to you.

Rule Summary: Analogies are claims that fall on the continuum from strong to weak. Stronger analogies are specific about how what is being compared is similar, and weaker analogies make claims of similarity where the differences are far greater.

Rule #11: Filter All Relevant Assumptions Through These Same Rules

If you take any claim and run it through the previous ten rules, you can still come to some wildly unreasonable conclusions. Consider the following claim:

Zeus' lightning bolt fuels the sun.

You might acknowledge how little you know about cosmology, and accept that you are biased in that you worship the Greek gods, including Zeus. The claim is clear and requires no isolation, but you might ask for clarity on what exactly is meant by "fuels the sun." The claim might be clarified as

Zeus' lightning bolt radiates energy that is solely responsible for keeping the sun burning.

This also takes care of probability, degree, and contributing factors. After careful consideration, although this is ultimately unfalsifiable, you find this claim plausible. Where did you go wrong? The claim contains the assumption that Zeus exists as well as his lightning bolt. Because you already accept this claim, every claim having to do with Zeus becomes more plausible. The solution is to unpack and dissect the assumptions that are contained within claims and run those through the same rules of reason.

A dose of reason is required when questioning assumptions. For example, we must question the existence of Zeus and his lightning bolt, but we don't need to question the existence of the sun. It may be the case that members of a Zeus cult would claim that it is "self-evident" that Zeus exists and not think to question that assumption. There is not much we can do about those folks besides remind them to review rule #1 again.

Rule Summary: Realize that claims often contain several other implied claims, many of which should also be run through the rules of reason.

Putting It All Together

In this final section, we'll take a look at several claims, and I'll run them through the eleven rules. As a reminder, the goal is not to determine the probability of the claim being true; it is to evaluate the strength of the claim, or if making the claim, ensure that it is strong. We do this by revising the claim throughout the process, building a stronger claim as we go. This works best as a cooperative process where all parties involved participate in the process to strengthen the claim.

A Bumper Sticker Claim

We'll start with a common claim/meme shared on the Internet:

Guns don't kill people; people kill people.

✓ **Acknowledge the Limits of Your Knowledge Regarding the Claim.** I never made or shared this claim, so I am not sure what people who do make this claim mean exactly. This admission prevents me from making a strawman out of the argument and prompts me to seek more information.

✓ **Explore Your Biases Related to the Claim.** I have no strong position on guns. I like shooting them, but I don't own one. I am left-leaning politically, but the gun debate is one of the least interesting to me of all political issues.

✓ **Isolate the Actual Claim.** There is an obvious implicit claim within this explicit claim. I can make assumptions if necessary, but the first choice is to ask for clarification from the person who made the claim. What do they mean, exactly? Do they mean restricting gun access won't make a difference in murders? Do they mean stricter gun laws won't make a difference in murders? Do they agree that restrictions will make a difference in murders, but that would infringe on their rights? We need clarification.

At this stage, we would ideally get a revised claim by the person who made the claim. Otherwise, we can continue by applying the following rules to all of the possible claims we propose. Let's assume the claim was revised to

Stricter gun laws violate our Constitutional rights.

✓ **Clearly and Precisely Define Each Relevant Term.** What are "Constitutional rights" specifically?

Stricter gun laws violate the Second Amendment, which is the

*right of the people to keep and
bear Arms, shall not be infringed.*

✓ **Use Terms That Reflect the Scope of
the Claim Accurately.** By defining
"Constitutional rights," we narrowed the
scope from what initially sounded much
more problematic to a specific amendment.

✓ **Operationalize Terms When Possible.**
There is no need to make any terms
measurable in our latest version of the
claim.

✓ **Make the Claim Falsifiable When
Possible.** This is ultimately a legal claim
that rests on a legal opinion. Falsification
would include a court of law ruling that this
is not the case. With such a politically-
charged topic, it is unlikely that everyone
would accept any court's legal opinion on
this issue, so making it objectively falsifiable
might be an impossibility.

✓ **Express an Accurate and Meaningful
Level of Confidence**. I would argue that
this is a case where a threshold is relevant.
Even if our rights are "violated a little" or
"kinda violated," it makes more sense to
keep a violation of rights as a binary
distinction so that we either take action or
don't. The extent of the violation can be on a
continuum, but the decision to take action
or not is the binary distinction.

✓ **Convert Causes to Contributing
Factors When Appropriate.** We can say
that stricter gun laws cause the violation,
which makes sense if the claim is true. The
gun laws don't "contribute to" the violation

in the claim; they are the only reason for it, according to the claim.

✓ **Make Strong Analogies and Call Out Weak Ones.** The claim does not use any analogies.

✓ **Filter All Relevant Assumptions Through These Same Rules.** One assumption here might be the meaning of "the right to bear Arms." Does "Arms" apply to semi-automatic weapons? If yes, how about fully-automatic weapons? Nuclear and chemical weapons? If we don't allow certain kinds of guns, why do we allow knives and even sticks? What is the rule here for where we draw the line?

At the very least, we moved from what is a very weak claim due mostly to its ambiguity:

Guns don't kill people; people kill people.

to a much stronger claim (as indicated by its clarity and precision) that lays the framework for a productive debate.

Stricter gun laws violate the Second Amendment, which is the right of the people to keep and bear Arms, shall not be infringed.

Going through the rules might have also prepared us to argue more objectively and fairly while reconsidering our relevant assumptions.

An Analogy

Analogies are claims in that they are claiming that one thing is like another thing in some way. Evaluating the strength of an analogy is evaluating the strength of the claim.

Here is a meme that has been widely circulated during the COVID-19 pandemic when new cases, hospitalizations, and death have started to slow, and many people were pushing to lift the restrictions put in place to slow the spread of the virus.

The curve is flattening; we can lift restrictions = The parachute has slowed our fall enough; we can take it off now.

✓ **Acknowledge the Limits of Your Knowledge Regarding the Claim.** I am not an epidemiologist, although I don't know how much that matters yet for this analogy. I do think we need to know the primary reason the restrictions were put into place, which I currently don't know.

✓ **Explore Your Biases Related to the Claim.** I am an optimist and have a strong, negative emotional reaction to pessimistic posts, headlines, and claims about COVID-19 that highlight worse-case scenarios and play on the fears of the public in order to affect behavior. I tend to unreasonably dismiss the doom and gloom associated with the virus and accept the positive news.

✓ **Isolate the Actual Claim.** If possible, we should ask those who share this analogy what exactly they mean by this. I don't have this luxury here, so I need to do my best to accurately isolate the claim being made without creating a strawman. The claim appears to be clear:

We should not lift the restrictions just because the curve is flattening.

This revised claim introduces *decision making* or evaluating suggested courses of action. This is beyond the scope of this book, so we will stick to the original analogy, especially if our goal is to simply determine the strength of the analogy rather than engage in an argument or debate.

✓ **Clearly and Precisely Define Each Relevant Term.** Does "The curve is flattening" refer to the fact that the number of daily new cases are being kept at a manageable level that is not overloading local healthcare systems, or does it mean it is approaching that point? Or does it mean something else? What is included, specifically, in "restrictions?"

✓ **Use Terms That Reflect the Scope of the Claim Accurately.** The phrase "lift restrictions" is missing the scope. Can we lift all restrictions? Some? Many? Most? This matters because the claim is that it is analogous to taking off a parachute (the extreme). By this, it would seem that "all" restrictions is what is meant.

✓ **Operationalize Terms When Possible.** The claim doesn't dispute the flattening of the curve, which is a term that we would generally want to operationalize. But in this case, it is not necessary—it is irrelevant to the claim/analogy.

✓ **Make the Claim Falsifiable When Possible.** Falsification doesn't apply to analogies, and if looking at the modified claim, it doesn't apply because the claim is an opinion.

✓ **Express an Accurate and Meaningful Level of Confidence**. This doesn't apply.

✓ **Convert Causes to Contributing Factors When Appropriate.** This doesn't apply.

✓ **Make Strong Analogies and Call Out Weak Ones.** Here is where we will do most of the work, given that this claim is an analogy. Recall the different meanings for "the curve is flattening." What is meant by this will determine how strong this analogy is. The parachute keeps us from dying a) while we are falling and b) as long as we have it on. Restrictions keep some people from dying (those who can't get treatment due to an overloaded healthcare system and possibly those who get the virus later when better treatment is available) while a) the local healthcare system would otherwise be overloaded and b) the restrictions are kept in place.

Is "the curve is flattening" more analogous to taking off the parachute while still falling or taking off the parachute after landing? Even if the curve has flattened and the local healthcare systems can manage the load, removing the restrictions might result in the overload still. If you take off a parachute after you landed, there is virtually no chance that you are still at risk of falling to your death.

Overall, I would say that this is a decent analogy, more on the side of strong than weak. Recall that strong claims are not necessarily true claims; the strength of the claim is independent of its veracity. Likewise, strong analogies that reduce to an opinion don't necessarily make for a good opinion.

✓ **Filter All Relevant Assumptions Through These Same Rules.** The main assumption here is that lifting restrictions while the curve is flattening / when the curve has flattened will result in a disaster analogous of taking off a parachute in mid-air. The other assumption is that leaving the restrictions in place will result in a better outcome than removing the restrictions. There also seems to be an assumption that "restrictions" are all or nothing, with no option to remove some restrictions while leaving others. These assumptions should be evaluated.

The Supernatural

A common misconception is that supernatural or *faith-based claims* are "beyond" reasoning when, in fact, the vast majority of faith-based claims are not immune to the scrutiny of good reasoning. Acknowledging the limits of your knowledge and exploring biases are rules that are perhaps even more relevant with these kinds of claims since people tend to have an even greater emotional commitment to faith-based claims. And many faith-based claims are still ultimately claims about the natural world—usually violations of natural law, which can be investigated scientifically and reasoned.

Let's apply these rules to one of the most common faith-based claims in the West:

Prayers work.

✓ **Acknowledge the Limits of Your Knowledge Regarding the Claim.** There isn't much here that requires any relevant knowledge.

✓ **Explore Your Biases Related to the Claim.** I am an atheist (i.e., I don't believe that any gods exist to answer prayers). However, I would love it if such a being existed.

✓ **Isolate the Actual Claim.** The claim is already isolated.

✓ **Clearly and Precisely Define Each Relevant Term.** What is prayer? Are we talking about a sort of meditative prayer or a petitionary prayer? Are we referring to praying for our own needs or those of others? To whom does the prayer need to be directed, if anyone? It may be the case the one making the claim is claiming that every kind of prayer works, as long as it is directed to the right being. This is a shotgun approach where so many claims are presented that they all cannot be addressed, so it is best to start by focusing on one clear and precise claim:

Asking a Catholic Saint to heal your physical body works.

What kind of physical ailments are we referring to, and how do we know when they are healed? Do severed limbs count? If not, why not?

Asking a Catholic Saint to cure your cancer works.

What is meant "works?" This seems like a term that needs to be operationalized.

✓ **Use Terms That Reflect the Scope of the Claim Accurately.** Does it work all the time? Sometimes? We can address this when we operationalize "works."

✓ **Operationalize Terms When Possible.** How do we measure "works?" How do we distinguish between healing through medical intervention and the effects of prayer? How do we distinguish between healing through passing time and the effects of prayer? How do we distinguish between spontaneous remission and the effects of prayer?

Asking a Catholic Saint to cure your cancer works as indicated by a statistically significant difference in recovery as

compared to those who don't pray.

✓ **Make the Claim Falsifiable When Possible.** The claim is falsifiable as it currently is written. The claim is not that a Catholic Saint is the one responsible for the healing, just that the process of asking a Catholic Saint for healing has a statistically significant effect. This is testable.

✓ **Express an Accurate and Meaningful Level of Confidence**. This has been addressed by operationalizing "works."

✓ **Convert Causes to Contributing Factors When Appropriate.** This claim is vague enough so that no cause is being claimed, but one is implied. The one making the claim might not want to go as far as to claim that there is a supernatural cause and may be fine with the conclusion that the cause can be psychosomatic —a placebo effect of sorts. Again, we never want to create a strawman of the claim, so get clarification if possible. Assume such clarification was offered:

Asking a Catholic Saint to cure your cancer results in the Catholic Saint facilitating the healing through God's power, as indicated by a statistically significant difference in recovery as compared to those who don't pray.

Although we took a step forward in the strength of the claim by being more specific as to the cause, we took a giant step back in strength by putting forth an unfalsifiable claim, that is, there is no way to demonstrate that the Catholic Saint facilitated the healing through God's power. Since this would effectively be a dead end, we might suggest leaving out the cause and moving forward to debate/investigate the more generic claim.

✓ **Make Strong Analogies and Call Out Weak Ones.** No analogies were used in this claim.

✓ **Filter All Relevant Assumptions Through These Same Rules.** The one making the claim might assume that Catholic Saints exist and can hear prayers, as well as that God exists and chooses to answer prayers. These are some significant assumptions that should be evaluated.

Conclusion

Claims are constantly being made, many of which are confusing, ambiguous, too general to be of value, exaggerated, unfalsifiable, and suggest a dichotomy when no such dichotomy exists. Good critical thinking requires a thorough understanding of the claim before attempting to determine its veracity. Good communication requires the ability to make clear, precise, explicit claims, or "strong" claims. The rules of reason in this book provide the framework for obtaining this understanding and ability.

While it may be a good idea to keep these rules handy as a checklist you can refer to when needed, repeated application of these rules will become a speedy unconscious process. You don't need to remember all the rules or the order in which I have them listed. The more you remember, however, the better equipped you will be.

The Eleven Rules of Reason for Making and Evaluating Claims

1. Acknowledge the Limits of Your Knowledge Regarding the Claim.

2. Explore Your Biases Related to the Claim.

3. Isolate the Actual Claim.

4. Clearly and Precisely Define Each Relevant Term.

5. Use Terms That Reflect the Scope of the Claim Accurately.

6. Operationalize Terms When Possible.

7. Make the Claim Falsifiable When Possible.

8. Express an Accurate and Meaningful Level of Confidence.

9. Convert Causes to Contributing Factors When Appropriate.

10. Make Strong Analogies and Call Out Weak Ones.

11. Filter All Relevant Assumptions Through These Same Rules.

About The Author

For Dr. Bennett's complete bio, other books, online courses, and websites, please visit http://www.bobennett.com.